Preface

Thank you for your interest in becoming a certified facilitator of The Exit Plan Program ("Exit Plan" or "Program"), a preparation guide for helping the incarcerated prepare for release. Each participant will prepare a personal reentry plan, and you will facilitate or set the stage for this process to happen.

To become a certified facilitator, you will participate in a webinar with Exit Plan's co-founders, Trina Frierson, Louise Grant and Jordan Lawhead ("co-founders") Upon certification you may:

- Teach Exit Plan in any U.S. correctional institution (with the co-founders' approval)

- Apply for grants or other funding to pay you for your services.[1]

Facilitators will use dialogue and writing exercises to help participants examine past decisions and to explore new possibilities upon release. The obstacles participants face upon release are real and overwhelming. Facilitators will use Exit Plan to identify these challenges and find solutions.

---

[1] Exit Plan facilitators volunteer their services, but this may change as the program expands.

The Story Behind Exit Plan

The Co-Founders

Trina Frierson is a former inmate, a recovered substance abuser and the founder and CEO of Mending Hearts, Inc., a nonprofit transitional living center in Nashville which provides services for more than 90 women.

Louise Grant is a 15-year veteran of the corrections industry with 13 years in corporate America serving in leadership roles in marketing and communications. She has volunteered and mentored incarcerated women in Nashville for over a decade.

Jordan Lawhead is a singer/songwriter, entrepreneur, and a cancer survivor. Intrigued by the stories of individuals who have overcome personal obstacles from disease, physical disabilities or incarceration, Jordan utilized his nonprofit, YouInspire, to produce videos detailing their stories and successes.

Louise's belief in the importance of strong reentry programs led to her collaboration with Jordan, and Trina. Louise and Jordan, inspired by Trina's journey, produced a video about her. The camaraderie that developed during the making of the video, led to further collaboration. In conjunction with other musicians, the co-founders sponsored a series of musical performances that were held at various jails and prisons. During these performances held in 2013-2014, Trina shared the story of her own incarceration, attributing much of her success to having an exit plan. Her message was simple, "You can succeed and change your life with the help of an exit plan." Trina's story and her commitment to helping the formerly incarcerated became the genesis for Exit Plan.

Exit Plan incorporates Trina's story into a practical twelve-chapter workbook. Exercises at the end of each chapter encourage clearer thinking and problem solving - skills essential to living outside jail or prison.

After its publication, Exit Plan was introduced to the staff at the Women's Correctional Development Center (CDC-F) as a tool to facilitate reentry and reduce recidivism. After incorporating suggestions from the Sheriff's Office, Exit Plan was approved by the CDC as a pilot program.

By the middle of 2015, Exit Plan was implemented. The initial class was comprised of approximately 20 incarcerated women who met with Trina, Louise and Jordan for two hours, twice weekly. Exit Plan ran for six-weeks and surpassed expectations. The CDC asked that Exit Plan be expanded to provide mentoring and aftercare services to participants after release. A former inmate who had worked at Mending Hearts took on the role of mentor.

Apart from teaching the Exit Plan, co-founders are developing a listserve and other supports for graduates of the program. They're also creating multi media content to supplement the chapter workbook. Jordan, who's producing the video component, is confident that emphasizing specific sections of the workbook will make Exit Plan even more effective. Grants and donations are expected to defray these production costs, including the printing of workbooks and training certified facilitators. As the program expands, Exit Plan will be implemented at other correctional facilities and taught by certified facilitators. We strongly believe that Exit Plan will be purchased as a self-study guide in both Spanish and English.

The Facilitator

By reading this manual, you have already demonstrated your wish to help the formerly incarcerated succeed after release. No special skills are needed to become a facilitator but facilitators are expected to:

- Have a clearly-set agenda for presenting each chapter of the workbook;

- Actively engage participants and keep them focused on the curriculum.

- Be prompt and prepared for class;

- Be understanding and flexible if a class must be cancelled;

- Be responsive to participants' questions.

The study questions will elicit intimate information about the participants' family lives and details about arrests and convictions. Facilitators must be receptive and non-judgmental towards Exit Plan participants when this kind of information is shared

Minimum Requirements for teaching the Exit Plan Program

Recommended class size: 12 participants per facilitator; up to 25 with two facilitators.

Program Gender: The Exit Plan may be taught to either females or males. Some of the information is more geared towards the female population, since Trina wrote the story from her personal perspective. However, the majority of the content is gender-neutral.

Length of a participant's remaining sentence: 2 months up to 1 year

Number of Curriculum Hours: A minimum of 18 and a maximum of 36 hours. The co-founders allocate 26 hours to teach Exit Plan, which includes a 2-hour graduation ceremony.

Number of Program Weeks: A minimum of 5 and a maximum of 8 weeks.

Number of Facilitators: a minimum of one. For large groups of up to 25, two or more facilitators are needed to drive discussion, offer different perspectives and keep the group on topic.

Material Covered Per Class: We recommend covering 1 entire chapter during each class period, which includes the study questions. Participants should be assigned the corresponding homework at the end of each chapter.

Materials Provided to Participants: Each participant shall receive: 1 Exit Plan workbook; a Pocket Folder with loose sheets of notebook paper to be used for any extra assignments or journal entries; a Name Tag for each class; and at least one writing pen. (All of these materials must be approved in advance by the primary contact person at the correctional facility.)

Best Practices for Teaching Exit Plan

Employing proven techniques will increase your effectiveness. Be as creative as possible in presenting the material. Interaction among participants is key and may result in profound change. Brainstorming, collaboration and role-playing enhance interaction and are excellent ways to present the material. You may facilitate interaction by using the following proven techniques:

Group Circle – Sitting in a circle is intimate and conducive to sharing;

Name Tags – Nametags help participants acknowledge each other more easily.

Be Friendly and Professional – This will help the group learn to trust and share personal information with you and the other participants.

Ice Breakers – Ice breakers ease communication. They are especially helpful in the beginning, and we recommend using them during the first few classes. As an example, have each participant choose a word that describes a personal positive quality. It should be a word the student identifies with and finds uplifting. Laughter often accompanies an ice breaker. Enjoy it. Humor is relaxing and creates a trusting environment.

Set Ground Rules – Have a list of guidelines that participants must follow. You might ask each participant to sign a personal contract to reinforce the commitment each participant is making to Exit Plan. Ground rules might include a maximum of two unexcused absences, or a promise not to disclose anything shared inside the classroom.

Meditation/Centering – Jails and prisons are loud and stressful. It's a good idea to begin each session with some quiet time, a guided meditation or breathing exercises. This will relax participants and help them focus on the chapters.

Participatory Reading – Each chapter begins with an excerpt of Trina's personal story. Invite each participant to read a few sentences or a paragraph aloud so everyone's involved. After reading the story, identify which parts resonate with the group and encourage discussion of it.

Discussion of Chapter Questions – Group discussion is critical. In fact, it's the foundation of Exit Plan. After reading the part of Trina's story that begins each chapter, institute some quiet time and ask the participants to answer the questions at the end of each chapter. The remainder of the session should be devoted to sharing and discussing the group's responses.

Visual Aids – Feel free to use poster boards, easels, chalkboards, or any other teaching tools to stimulate the group. Many people are visual learners and these aids will help generate answers and feedback. If you have access to an overhead projector or a DVD player, we encourage you to present a video, graph or chart to supplement the written material. We ask that you share any videos and visual aids with the co-founders prior to introducing them in class. We don't want to burden you but please be mindful of our obligation to ensure that materials comply with Exit Plan's mission. We support and applaud your efforts to enhance Exit Plan and want the program to reach as many people as possible.

Homework Assignments – Assign the chapter homework questions at the end of each class. You should begin each class with a discussion of the previous session's homework questions. After that, have the participants take turns reading Trina's story in the following chapter. You may supplement the homework by asking participants to draft journal entries or to think about how they will implement Exit Plan in their own lives upon release.

Guest Speakers – Some jails and prisons may permit visits by guest speakers. Guests can include someone who was previously incarcerated, a felon-friendly employer, or a representative from a state or local agency that assists former offenders. Guests can provide encouragement and important information about services available to participants upon release.

Access to Local Resources – Participants often have nowhere to go after they're released. They'll need help finding housing, jobs and transportation. We have compiled a list of organizations that provide services to the formerly incarcerated and ask that you update it with any additional providers that exist in your community. Providers include halfway houses, felon-friendly employers, food banks, clothing closets, bus transportation and access to medical services. Probation offices, local community centers and churches are good sources of information and may have suggestions for you to share with participants. We hope you'll continue to be a source of strength and hope to your students long after their release.

Graduation – Prepare graduation certificates and host a graduation ceremony for the class. Invite participants to speak about why the program was helpful and how their thinking has changed. If they choose to speak, allot about three minutes each. Ask the Director of Community Affairs, or the Chaplain, or whoever is responsible for the volunteer efforts at your correctional facility whether family members or friends can attend the graduation.

You are the spark that can foster change. You can help women believe in themselves and in their ability to succeed after release. Bring your talents, your skills and most of all, bring your heart to class- They'll love you for it.

Disabilities/Special Needs

Be sensitive to any disabilities or special needs in your group. Some participants may be illiterate, have a speech impediment or may struggle with a medical condition that makes reading or writing particularly difficult. Address the issue with a case manager to determine if the student is capable of fully participating in Exit Plan.

Bringing Exit Plan to Correctional Settings

Certified facilitators may teach Exit Plan in any correctional facility, halfway house addiction, or other treatment center. Although participation in Exit Plan is voluntary at this time, it possibly may become a mandatory program at some point. It is our hope that Exit Plan will be shared with as many people as possible to maximize their opportunities for success upon release.

If you'd like to bring Exit Plan to a facility where it is not being offered, please reach out to the chaplain, the volunteer coordinator or the head of programs at the jail or prison. Try to arrange a personal meeting or conference call during which you can present Exit Plan and answer questions about it. The co-founders would be happy to participate or help you draft a proposal if necessary.

Many correctional facilities require that volunteer programs be evidence based. We recognize this and are using scientific methodology such as meta-analysis to evaluate the cognitive patterns of Exit Plan participants. It is well established that internal transformation will shift thinking and decision-making. Meditation has also been found to change cognitive thinking and patterns.

Post Exit Plan

We encourage you to mentor former participants and to keep abreast of services available in your community for the formerly incarcerated. Government agencies, nonprofits and for-profit businesses are all good sources of information.

Copyright

Institutions and agencies may not photocopy Exit Plan curriculum without the express permission of the Co-founders. All participants must be provided with their own printed workbook.

www.ingramcontent.com/pod-product-compliance
Lightning Source LLC
Chambersburg PA
CBHW060430010526
44118CB00017B/2435